The
Junk Man's MBA

*Lessons from my dad on living
and working in times of rapid change*

ANNETTE
MOSER-WELLMAN

For my father,

Alan Malloy Moser who was the engine of the
business and

For my mother,

Elizabeth Eileen Moser who was the fuel

I am the daughter of a Junk Man. Alan Moser would introduce himself that way. He was a proud auto wrecker—a scrappy entrepreneur who made his living salvaging used cars, trucks, ships, and more. He was a man's man—hacking out a living under the chassis of an 18-wheeler in the driving Seattle rain. And even though feelings weren't his native language, we knew he loved us. His success year after year provided for our family. But more than that, he shared his love with a constant stream of business advice: how to make a business run, how to make it grow, and how to manage an unpredictable future.

As life would have it, I became an entrepreneur as well. My experience was wholly different from my dad's. I earned an MBA from one of the best business schools in the world. Over fifteen years ago, I founded an innovation consultancy. From Microsoft to Coca-Cola, my firm has given advice to leading companies on how to grow in the midst of accelerating change. Ironically, the lessons I learned from my dad in the junk business are becoming more and more relevant to all areas of work. Change comes so fast anymore you feel like a cat caught in the dryer fighting to get equilibrium. From high job turnover to new skills demanded and six small business owners for every corporate job, stability is a thing of the past. Because *the pace of change itself is changing,* you have to learn to be scrappy and flexible—making everything you've got work to keep moving ahead. The business wisdom of the wrecking yard has now become the tenets of the boardroom.

This book shares Al's Junk Man's MBA—his street-smart business principles—with you. Alan died when I was twenty-five, yet his "mental download" has guided my thinking and informs my company's work with clients today. I'll give you a peek under the hood of how business folks need to think like salvagers—doing more with less and dealing with increasing magnitudes of change and uncertainty. This is a short book. Daddy would have wanted it that way. Never a big reader, he graduated high school by a whisker because he almost flunked typing. Yet his entrepreneurial success proves that "smart" has no correlation to fancy degrees and that creativity is the key to winning. In the years ahead, each of us will need to think of ourselves as entrepreneurs.

ONE DAY CHICKEN, THE OTHER DAY FEATHERS.

GENERAL AUTO WRECKING CO.
WE PAY CASH FOR CARS AND TRUCKS
AUTO AND TRUCK PARTS
1436 LEARY WAY
SEATTLE, WASHINGTON 98107

The salvaging business is not sexy. General Auto Wrecking was a retail storefront, where people would come in for used car and truck parts. Daddy also owned a larger yard outside the city where he would haul cars to crush into scrap for sale. Grease always covered his hands. To wash up at the end of the day, he would scrub his face with gasoline. I never saw his fingernails clean until we had been on a long vacation.

Dad's business transactions came in two streams: smaller sales from car and truck parts and larger sales from buying used trucks and machinery and reselling them at a higher price. His first job was selling newspapers at thirteen. He saved his meager profits and bought his first car. He overhauled it and sold it for a profit. He learned the art of buying low, improving a product, and reselling higher. He got comfortable with the cycle of irregular cash flow. When it was a good day at the yard, he'd come home and say, "One day chicken, the other day feathers."

On a bad day, he'd say exactly the same thing. What he meant was that income was inherently unpredictable in a world of making it on your own. He was admonishing us. Get comfortable with being uncomfortable. He learned a certain even-keelness about life as an entrepreneur.

Being comfortable with being uncomfortable is the new form of learning to do business globally. Few of us will have jobs where we can be secure for ten or twenty years. Most of us will need new skill sets every three to five years to keep pace with innovation. Exponential change in technology markets will mean a higher level of fluctuation in jobs and the employment market. We will all need to think like entrepreneurs and accept the new way of working that goes along with it.

A client recently told me that the uncertainty of his position amidst layoffs and restructures was making it hard for him to concentrate on doing good work. As empathetically as I could, I told him to "Get over it." Find ways to deliver help however you can. Look for someone around you that sees the value in what you do. A simple test to see if what you do is valuable is to ask yourself, "If I was running my own company selling what I do everyday here, what would I be selling?"

Security no longer lies within our job but within our own abilities—our knowledge base, our talents, and most of all, our creativity. Confidence comes in knowing that we can make it out there no matter what. We need to practice being content in times of plenty and times of want. We can plan our lives and even our finances that way. Accepting that income will be there sometimes and sometimes not gives you freedom. Freedom to save well. You may not have chicken every day, but when you do, put some in the freezer. And freedom to play well. Enjoy those times when you are between work to build your skills and enjoy life.

Most entrepreneurs love what they do. It's real. It's not an abstraction. They produce value. They know exactly what they deliver and see the potential for opportunity in making more than a paycheck. From recycling junk cars to writing computer code, being uncomfortable is the cost of doing business and there is a certain thrill there. We may not love the pressure, but we can learn to live with it and celebrate ourselves as leaders in the new reality of work.

Roll around in uncertainty. Uncertainty helps you see opportunity and get new ideas for how to create 'chicken'. Uncertainty is your best and most trusted teacher.

YOU'VE GOT TO GET SOMETHING GOING FOR YOU.

I told you that my dad would introduce himself as "Al Moser, the Junk Man." But he also would joke around the house that he was "Al Moser, Counselor at Law." He had a sense that if circumstances had been different, he might have had a different future. He would have been insanely unhappy as a lawyer and he knew it, but he liked to make fun of what he perceived as the cushy life—a profession that didn't require being a scrappy entrepreneur.

What was he talking about when he said, "You've got to get something going for you?" This bit of wisdom is the one that took me the longest to understand. I knew it was business advice, but its meaning was opaque and mysterious. I'm not proud to say that I perceived many of my dad's principles as naïve or maybe even uneducated. From a young age, I wanted to marry someone who wore a tie to work—an implicit rejection of his life in coveralls and his way of making a living. I loved the life of the mind, excelling at my studies and dreaming of the life of ideas. I even married a scholar.

Only through my deep consulting and coaching work with senior executives did I find the first thread of what he meant. The folks I met who were successes in the highest corporate ranks of business were smart. Leaders of tech companies, restaurant chains, and manufacturing firms were well educated and prided themselves on their brains and analytical abilities. But at the end of the day, I learned they weren't that much smarter than the rest of us. Like the great physicist Richard Feynman said, "We are not that much smarter than each other."

More than smart, these business people were lucky. They were born into a life that afforded them education and access. Even intellect is a function of luck. Sure, they worked hard, but there were others working as hard who were not as lucky. The agency of luck has a powerful way of leveling the field—making us realize we are not that special. Still, we have a habit of ascribing power to those who are luckier than we are. Much of the dysfunction of corporate leadership comes from masking the fear that someone will pull back the curtain and realize a prime mover in their success has been luck.

Dad embraced the rapid change inherent in the junk business because he knew that the randomness and messiness of it all gave him a higher chance of being lucky. Who knew what people might want to buy or sell that day? Or what surprising items might come up at auction? When the pace of change accelerates around you it's easier to find little openings for new opportunities. You can lure luck your way by creating something new wherever you are.

"Getting something going for you" means being productive in the highest sense of the word. It's working in service of your best work. What matters is your creative output. It's what you build with your own hands that develops success. From making an engine work to producing a new form of energy or creating a new marketing idea, understanding what you can create is central to moving ahead in the future.

I call the value you bring to the marketplace your intellectual capital. What is your unique body of knowledge? Do you know how to direct videos? Do you create new social marketing ideas? Do you know the art of understanding people? Do you know how to serve people well? What is your unique set of gifts? This is your intellectual capital, what you can trade in the entrepreneurial world.

Now, if you're like many, you're thinking, I don't know what's unique about me. In our innovation consultancy work, I've learned most people don't perceive themselves as creative. Virtually one-hundred percent of kindergartners self-identify as creative when only thirty percent of seventh graders do. By the time we start working creativity has been educated out of us. We consistently underestimate what we know and what we can create. I've had incredibly talented people confess to me they don't feel as smart or as creative as others. We don't know how great we really are. Our problem is not too much pride, but not enough of it. Not too much ego strength, but not enough.

I encourage clients to write a list of their own unique intellectual capital. If you could patent you, what would you be protecting? If you packaged up what you "produce" every day and sold it on a freelance talent website, who would buy it? You have more skills and talents than you know.

What's your intellectual capital? What can you get going for yourself?

SHOOT A SHOTGUN
AND NOT A RIFLE.

I knew my dad was disappointed he had two
girls and no boys. It must have been lonely for

him. We loved to dress Barbies. He loved to hunt with guns. We loved to chat with friends on the phone. He wanted to ride horses silently. I used to think these gender differences were nurtured, until a friend of mine had a boy. When she told him he could have no toy guns, the five-year-old bit the shape of a gun from his peanut butter sandwich and began shooting.

But I learned to love skeet shooting with Daddy. He taught me the technique of preparing the shotgun, holding it, and aiming. He taught me how to anticipate the trajectory of the clay pigeon. He explained that the spray of pellets ensures a better hit rate than the single bullet of a rifle. I was good at shooting and consistently beat him. He never lived long enough to see my business success, but this was one small area I could see his pride shine.

In our innovation consulting work, we often counsel clients to shoot a shotgun in the uncertain landscape of business. When the pace of change is accelerating, it becomes increasingly difficult if not impossible to anticipate the future. So experimentation becomes the rule of the day. You have to shoot a gun with a lot of pellets in the shot to increase the probability you will hit a target. Companies large and small have to rely on a set of tests—small bets that increase the likelihood of success in some area, such as launching into a new country, targeting a different consumer, or building a new product line. Successful companies build robust but lightweight products and services then iterate quickly to see what sticks.

That's what scrappy junk dealers have always done: identify areas of need they can fill even in small ways and then see what has staying power even if just for a little while. Often with little money to spend, they try something and see if it has momentum and catches on. They have several experiments in the mix. I remember when Daddy's scrap metal business was taking off, he didn't have time to help people through the yard, but he often told them that they could search for parts in his yard and come to him with what they found. He was focusing on shooting the shotgun, and the scrap metal business soon eclipsed the profits from car parts.

I was in the advertising industry for many years until I started my own company in 1997. I had a dream I would write and sell a book on innovation. I knew I had a good idea and wanted to share it with the world. But after a couple of months, I realized getting a publisher would take longer than our savings would allow. So I decided to turn the concepts of the book into a workshop. I reached out to a friend and she ran the course as a free pilot at her company. That gave me the confidence and experience to shop the idea around to many different people.

It wasn't long before I had a viable business. I could have never predicted what it would have become. It was almost as if the business had a life of its own and I was just following in the wake of its boat. Later I did get the book published. A colleague who I shared the idea with early on said, "Wow. And to think you and I were just talking about this as a PowerPoint presentation just a few years ago!"

One of the tenants of the Junk Man's MBA is that we need to pursue several good ideas at the same time. When things in the marketplace are messy, disorganized, and uncertain, we have to focus on more ideas rather than fewer. We need to nurse many different projects that we believe have merit. The way to achieve success is to juggle many projects, experiment well and strive for new revenue streams. That's what an entrepreneur does – keeps creating new businesses to maximize the power of change.

Dream about what you can sell. Create a basket of experiments. Ask others about your ideas. If one or two don't work, no harm, no foul. Replace them with something new. Just keep moving ahead. Momentum is more important. Once you have some data points under your belt—what worked and what didn't—you can anticipate what the next thing might be. We make our biggest mistakes when we refuse to shoot.

WHAT'S THE NEXT BIG DEAL?

I've spent a lot of time in the rarefied air of
corporate conference rooms. There I hear a

lot of talk about strategy. And much of it is that—just talk. A Junk Man's MBA has no patience for talk without action. Because business for the Junk Man is a game. We may use a strategy, but we don't have a strategy. The bias is toward action—looking ahead to what the next opportunity could be and going for it. My dad would call these the *big deals*—the ideas that shook out from the basket of experiments as game-changing winners.

In the close quarters of home, Daddy would mumble under his breath, almost like a prayer, "What's the next big deal?" His imagination was always cogitating on the next big opportunity. Creating opportunity was his art.

In addition to the smaller profits he made on parts and scrap, he always had one or two big items he wanted to sell. If a ship caught his eye at auction, he'd buy it and immediately start calling his potential buyers. He drove thousands of miles to Alaska to buy equipment like a used 18-wheeler, repair it, and deliver it to a buyer. He always had a basket of industrial properties he wanted to buy and resell. If you could have looked deep into that brain, you would have seen the transactions populating the synapses like flashes of brilliance.

Ask my dad what the long-term vision for General Auto Wrecking was and he would have looked at you as if you had three heads. A typical business consultant will claim that not having a long-term vision is a mistake, but in the new reality of accelerated change, Alan had it right. It's the obsession with the near-term vision that really is the most fruitful. The writer,

E. L. Doctorow described this vision best, "When driving a car at night you can only see as far as the headlights shine."

Increasingly, we will all be driving our cars at night. Uncertainty about the long-term direction of work will be the rule and not the exception. Planning cycles will get shorter and shorter. Who knows what industries computer technology, robotics, and the like will spawn. The question that really matters is "What is the small vision at the end of your headlights?" In other words, what is your next big deal?

A client asked for my advice and counsel on her next job move. She was certain that her job description was going to be eliminated. She wanted to stay with the company, so she started interviewing for other open positions in the firm. I encouraged her to stop thinking about the positions posted but instead about the opportunities she saw around her—for customers, clients, internal folks, and her boss. If she could focus on the opportunities, she might uncover a big deal—a place to make a big impact. She asked one supplier if they could use a trained, inside sales person who really understood the client needs. They jumped at the chance and she found herself a new role as a sales person. She flexed her entrepreneurial muscle.

Stop thinking about getting a job. A job is where you sell your time. There is no financial advantage in selling time. You have a finite amount of it and it will always cap at an hourly rate. A job is an old industrial economy model.

Rather, think about selling products, services, and ideas. What basket of things can you sell in your current role and outside of it? What are the next big deals you see ahead for yourself and in the marketplace? What is the vision in your minds' eye for your life and work?

Start scouting opportunities. Start praying the Alan Moser prayer: "What is the next big deal?" Who knows, you may get an answer.

YOU GOTTA SWEAT IT OUT OF YOU.

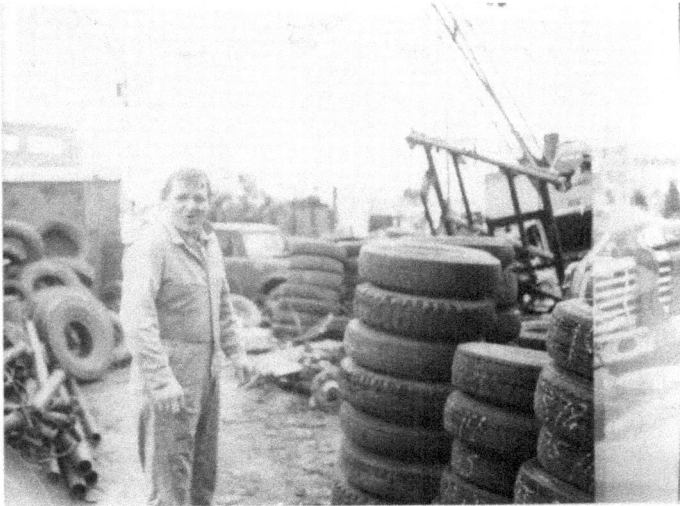

No one worked harder than my dad did. He left the house early before we went to school.

Mom called herself a short-order cook because she'd make a second meal for him when he came home late at night. He worked Saturday, as it was a big retail day. Sunday he would often go back to work or ride horses he housed at his Snohomish junk yard. Mom would joke that the wrecking yard was my dad's playpen.

He was an athlete. Every night he would do forty chin-ups "the hard way," with wrists turned toward his body. He would take two weeks out of every winter to pack horses into the Blue Mountains of Oregon alone. We would wait for him to come home with an elk head on the back of his pickup and a load of meat. When he had the flu, he'd take aspirin and go to the yard to weld. He always said, "When you are sick you gotta sweat it out of you." Maybe bad medical advice, but it worked for him.

Entrepreneurs are driven. Who can say where this intensity comes from, but it characterizes the life of entrepreneurs. They are working with their whole selves on the line. I used to think that some of us had this drive and others didn't. But I've learned drive is really a function of your set of expectations. It's about being so honest with yourself that you realize you can't rely on others to create things for you. You have to bet on yourself. If you think that you can accomplish something great, you can and will. If you think you can't, you won't. Drive is a daily choice.

In a way, good business people are good poets. We want to wrestle things down to the ground and force our work to mean something, to matter. Just as a poet fights for exactly the right image or word to express an encounter with life, so the entrepreneur's drive comes from making the business image a reality. They operate with the singular conviction that the work matters and, so, must be accomplished. Sweat is expected and required.

Failure is expected and required. The Junk Man plans for lost effort, dead-ends, and missed opportunities. Innovation requires waste, and the Junk Man knows this well. Some things sell, many things don't. The yard is an amalgam of hopes gone south and dreams hidden under a dark chassis. But there is no shame here. In environments of rapid change, failure is most welcome.

A year or so before iTunes launched, my consulting company ventured into a podcast business that provided a menu of different topics from leadership to spiritual growth. We worked hard to get original content from the best authors and produced a great offering of knowledge. It proved to be a good idea, so good in fact that Apple launched a podcast library bigger and better than what we even had in mind. A classic failure on our part—time and money piled in the junk yard. But in retrospect, we learned a lot from the misstep that helped our company grow in the future. We sweated that one out and lost, but it only increased the drive to keep charging on.

Working hard even in the midst of failure is satisfying because you know you are creating, and when you are creating, you are truly living.

IF YOU WANT SOMETHING DONE RIGHT, YOU'VE GOT TO DO IT YOURSELF.

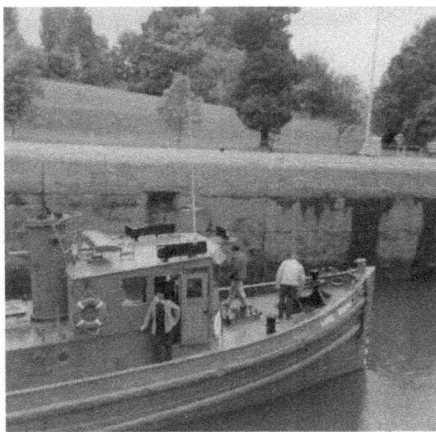

Collaboration is the trendy topic these days. The business guru's are telling us we need to create high-functioning teams and that genius ideas don't come to lone individuals. I disagree and think my dad would as well.

We are becoming a workforce less like company men and more like serial entrepreneurs. There is more responsibility for each person to deliver ideas and work directly on projects. No team representatives or managers anymore. Even in a very large firm, a VP told me, "We expect everyone to work on vital projects, including me. No *managers* here. We all have to come to a project with our own ideas to share."

It's time to reignite the power of the individual. Inspiration always comes in units of one. Ideas are mitigated through the imagination of one person. Intense partnership with two or three individuals or even a larger team can be very helpful in commercializing products and services, but we need to start taking responsibility for our own creative mind. We still say some are creative and others aren't—that notion in the new age of scrappy work is dead. Each of us needs to innovate.

Ralph Waldo Emerson, the great voice of American individualism had a lot to say about the power of individual genius. Listen to his work called Self-Reliance: "To believe your own thought, to believe what is true for you in your private heart is true for all...that is genius... Nothing is at last sacred but the integrity of your own mind."

In our consulting practice, we often hear a big cry for mentoring. "We want a mentoring culture where people share ideas with each other and guide each other." I tell clients there comes a time when you stop looking for a mentor. You realize you have to lead yourself. You have to become your own mentor. This shocks people.

Now I'm not advocating for a bunch of brilliant jerks running around a company, disconnected teams trampling each other, or dying on a vine without asking for help and advice. But it's time we recognize that we need to get our pioneering mojo back. Like my dad's wisdom, if we want something done right, we need to do it ourselves. We can't rely on others, the company, or the government to take care of us. We have to take back our imagination—the care of our own creative genius. We have to nurture our ideas and be the leaders who then nurture others by the power of our kick-it spirit.

In some sense we will need to be become serial entrepreneurs—creating one new business after the next. From research scientists to fashion designers, from internet start-ups to retailing concepts, as the pace of change quickens we will all be getting closer and closer to the transaction of business. There will be fewer institutions to protect us from the rapid ups and downs of the marketplace.

The good news is we are now working at the nub of what it means to be human—using our personal genius. Our creativity is the thin, but all-important layer, that separates us from computer intelligence. The human longing for meaning in work is found in creative contribution.

The Industrial Age and its systematic production stripped us of our sense of accomplishment in making things. We didn't see the work from beginning to end. Think of the next era as the "Salvage Age." The Salvage Age ushers in a new kind of radically important work that requires us to create something from very little—to utilize our personal genius. We can follow the trajectory of a project—including its messiness and failure—that reminds us what we, as individuals, are capable of accomplishing. There is a certain sense of relief in being the one who creates the idea and changes the ink cartridge at the same time.

Radical independence: when you start believing in yourself and your ideas, where does your imagination take you?

YOU'VE GOTTA CON THE CON.

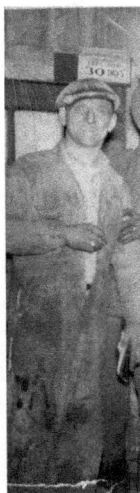

My dad worked day after day with people who sold him cars or trucks that he would turn around and repair or resell as parts. People would walk in off the street and ask him to buy things for cash. He got good at sifting truth from fiction. Did that transmission really work as well as the guy said it did? Was the price for the scrap metal fair? Dad was wise about human nature. He could spot a half-truth a mile away. He would tell me his strategy was to con *them*. I thought this sounded mercenary. But later I figured out what he meant. His strategy was this: simple honesty. He surprised people by telling the truth. I saw him negotiate countless times by saying things like, "I know you think it works, but let me show you why it doesn't. It will take me time to repair it. I'll buy it for half of what you are selling it for." Or "I just saw a similar property for sale at 5 percent less a square foot. Let me tell you why the other lot is a better deal for me." He offered a window into a real relationship—an honest transaction. His genuineness was disarming.

We face more cons in the digital marketplace than ever before. How many times have you heard, "Your call is important to us" and then been left in the electronic phone tree for hours? Or been offered something free online only to have your e-mail spammed with offers for products you didn't want. Even social networks dupe us by saying our data forms an anonymous "social graph," but privacy experts tell us that our digital trails and preferences are so unique, individual activity can easily be located.

It's clear we've handed over to computer intelligence one of the few jobs it can never do—be empathic. There is a glaring unmet need for personal, human compassion. A new demand for what makes people, people—spontaneous solutions, creativity in real time, caring, ideas with wisdom and, above all, honesty.

Our company's landline telephone rep was helping us reconfigure our services. It was a joy to work with him because he was on our side in the transaction: "Here's an idea, what if you...," "I think we can save you money if we changed...," or "Here's my direct number, don't hesitate to call me back." He knew that his honesty with us would help save the account. He had to be scrappy, think on his feet, and use his creative genius to figure out what we truly needed.

I like to challenge clients to practice inverting the Golden Rule. What would be different in your life and work if you could figure out how to "do unto" others as *they* would like to be "done unto." We often enter unconsciously into relationships with the expectation that others want to be served the same way we do. Our intentions may be good, but figuring out what other people want is often much more difficult. It requires a facility with love.

As Joseph Campbell, the great scholar of mythology, pointed out, "Technology is not going to save us. Our computers, our tools, our machines are not enough. We have to rely on our intuition, our true being." Instead of expecting humans to serve technology, a great opportunity exists to use technology to serve people.

How can you inject more humanness in how you serve people at work and beyond? How can you have dialog that is more honest with the people around you? How can you build your business that focuses on the unmet human needs you notice?

Become a master of relationships. Challenge yourself to be an expert in love.

HYAKU!

My dad left his auto-wrecking business for
a time to serve in the Korean War. He was a
sergeant in the infantry. Hard combat shaped

his toughness and his tough mindedness. He was ruggedly optimistic and relentlessly resourceful. When business was bad, he'd be down for a time, but had a resilience to bounce back. He didn't ruminate or worry much. He'd feel bad for a bit and stomp around, sure, but then he'd find something new to chase. In the midst of the sour deal or the persistent trough, he would find another challenge. He would scour around for something to sell, buy another property, or sell something in inventory—take a risk.

Perhaps it was the field of combat itself, or maybe it was there all along, but the Far East intensified his love of risk taking. He told stories about furloughs in Japan and gambling escapades. He learned the word "hyaku" in Japanese, meaning to throw down a $100 bet.

I learned that sometimes he won and many times he lost, but he was optimistic about his chances.

Whenever my dad was excited about a big deal, he would yell "Hyaku" around the house. It was a celebratory acknowledgement that he was alive, vital, in the game. He loved betting and knew that his business wouldn't grow—he wouldn't grow—unless he was able to keep making bets. He didn't care so much if he won; he always had many deals going at one time. It was the law of averages. Sooner or later something would pop.

When he won, he knew how to celebrate. Many of our family trips were big surprises. "Pack your bags. We are going to Disneyland tonight!" We'd load up the station wagon and drive all the way from Seattle to Anaheim—spontaneously finding places to stay along the way.

In times of exponential change, our tendency is to hunker down and try to wait things out until normalcy returns. We tend to shy away from betting because we think risk taking is unsafe and we want security and stability in our lives. Early in my career at an advertising agency someone told me that the best way to get promoted was to keep my head down and not take any chances.

Today we need to do the exact opposite—take risks, jump into something new, create lots of surprising ideas. Exponential change means the cycle of business will continue to speed up and we will experience more uncertainty. The only way to keep pace and have a chance at anticipating the future is to create.

That's why the junk business is such a good place for us to learn how to deal with change. Salvagers are famous for using very little money or resources to turn a profit. They forage through other people's leftovers and find what they can reuse, recycle, and repurpose. They start at the bottom of the business cycle rather than at the top. They know that in a fast-churn business environment, many valuable things get thrown off along the way—materials, resources, products, ideas that can be rekindled. By salvaging the half-life of what is "used" they create an entirely new value stream. They take risks by finding things that still have usefulness.

In the Salvage Age, garbage is holy and waste can be righteous. What is eBay but a massive recycling center? What is Microsoft's plan for home heating by redistributing server farms but salvaging energy? What is old can become new. The junkyard is an ecosystem of innovation.

What risks can you take in service of your genius? How can you celebrate the Salvage Age?

I'M LIVIN' BUT I'M DYIN'.

Paradox is the great revealer of opportunity. The most profound wisdom in life is both true and untrue at the same time. For example, we need to love our kids unconditionally, but we need to impose expectations to help them grow. We need to take care of the needs of others around us, but we need to take care of ourselves as well. When we sit back and ask ourselves what the two sides of any wisdom are, we develop a respect for the paradox. In the back and forth consideration of the two sides, we are transformed. Jesus taught using parables because the stories themselves forced a personal transformation. The parables thrust people into thinking differently about what was right in front of them. It's often in the midst of a paradox that a new idea or invention is born.

Daddy would often say, "I'm livin' but I'm dyin'." This paradox fascinated him. He knew it represented an important opportunity. Limits on his life forced him to live life as an adventure.

He was free to follow his dreams. Steve Jobs famously talked about the knowledge of his impending death as the ultimate catalyst for creativity.

We tend to spend our mental energy focusing on our limits or avoiding thinking about them at all. We try to angle past them or blame them on someone else. In the same way, we want to avoid thinking about the "trash" in our lives—the relationships that went awry, the bad business deals, the lost dreams. But it's in the paradox bounded by the limitations that new ideas are born. We need to view ourselves honestly to create something new. Yes, we are limited. Yes, we have many possibilities in front of us.

One of the beauties of the digital world is that we have even greater chances to create—to pen our novels, make our inventions, direct our own videos—the list goes on. Creativity is becoming the key currency. It's the natural gift we all have and increasingly don't need any intermediaries to use it. It means we are truly competing based on our talents, our character, and our creative vision. Creativity is *the* stuff we are made of.

My dad died at the age of fifty-five from an aggressive brain tumor. It was the final hunt of his life. He battled like he was back in Korea, with all the resourcefulness he had. He sought the best experimental treatments. He persevered through painful surgeries and seizures. He believed he could beat it. In the midst of it all, he told me, "There are so many more things I haven't done yet."

For most, these "things" would be trips to Europe or other far-flung places, fine meals, or great times with people. But for my dad, it probably meant more big deals down at the wrecking yard. His work was the place where he worked out his salvation with fear and trembling. The junk yard was the place he found his passion and played the game of finding an opportunity wherever it raised its head. Perhaps the singular truth about his life was that he **lived**.

Figure out what the opportunities are that are being born around you. Focus on the paradoxes. They will guide you. Life will always be petals and thorns. So in the words of Albert Camus— "create dangerously." It's the only way to be sure you have truly lived.

ABOUT ANNETTE MOSER-WELLMAN

Annette Moser-Wellman is one of the world's leading experts on innovation. Her company, FireMark Inc., works with leaders of Fortune 500 firms to create market breakthroughs. She has taught thousands of business managers how to use her model for creative thinking and apply it to develop new products and services. Ms. Moser-Wellman's clients include The Coca-Cola Company, Starbucks Coffee Company, Disney, Expedia, Microsoft, and many more.

Based on her research of creative genius in the arts and sciences, Ms. Moser-Wellman's book *The Five Faces of Genius: Creative Thinking Styles to Succeed at Work (Viking/Penguin)* demonstrates how business people can learn to invent from the greats of history. She developed a profiling tool to assist managers in understanding their personal creative style and become inventors.

In addition to speaking engagements for corporate and public audiences, Ms. Moser-Wellman consults with firms on bringing innovation to organizations. She works with management to optimize creativity and develop new ideas for today's rapidly changing marketplace. She specializes in finding the intersection between future trends and new business invention. Her proprietary process, *The*

Legacy Project, coaches leaders on how to utilize their personal genius to reinvent their firms and their markets.

Ms. Moser-Wellman has conducted research on innovation and technology for Northwestern University's Media Management Center. She is a guest lecturer at the University of Chicago's Booth School of Business. She produces papers, webinars, and blogs on the intersection of technology and media.

Ms. Moser-Wellman holds an MBA from the University of Chicago and a Master of Divinity from Princeton Theological Seminary. Her undergraduate degree was in art and she has had an abiding interest in the lives of creative individuals. She lives with her husband and two daughters in the Seattle area. Ms. Moser-Wellman's passion is to help others find their genius and use it to transform the world.